What School Secretaries Do When No One Is Looking

by Jim Grant and
Irv Richardson

Illustrated by Patrick Belfiori

Published by
Crystal Springs Books • Peterborough, New Hampshire
1-800-321-0401

What School Secretaries Do When No One Is Looking
by Jim Grant and Irv Richardson.
Illustrated by Patrick Belfiori

Published by Crystal Springs Books, Ten Sharon Road, PO Box 500, Peterborough, NH 03458.
Phone 1-800-321-0401
Fax 1-800-337-9929

ISBN 1-884548-23-7

To Barbara Heck, one of the most
supportive parents, and a world class school secretary
who willingly helped everyone – even
when no one was looking.

— Jim Grant

To Kathy Sullivan, who finally got her
dream job helping children and staff
as a school secretary.

— Irv Richardson

To Mom, Dad, and Gail. Thank you.

—Patrick Belfiori

Special Thanks to
Dick Dunning
for his contribution to this book.

NATIONAL SECRETARY
Mrs. Heck
THANK YOU!!
Mrs. Heck for all that you've done for us!
Lorraine
Jim
Kate
Mark
Ron
Patrick
Irv
Mrs. Grant
Jen
Gail
Luther
Mr. Rosen
Michele
Tommy
Thank YOU!

School secretaries deliver mail.

School secretaries mentor new staff.

School secretaries move furniture.

School secretaries are tour guides.

School secretaries cover recess.

School secretaries make loans.

School secretaries direct traffic.

School secretaries sell things.

School secretaries stay late.

School secretaries repair.

School secretaries comfort.

School secretaries intercept angry parents.

School secretaries type . . .

and type . . . and type . . . .

School secretaries find out-of-stock supplies.

School secretaries handle multiple tasks.

School secretaries watch kids grow.

School secretaries babysit.

And while no one is looking
school secretaries make life a little easier.